WHAT'S INSIDE?

BOATS

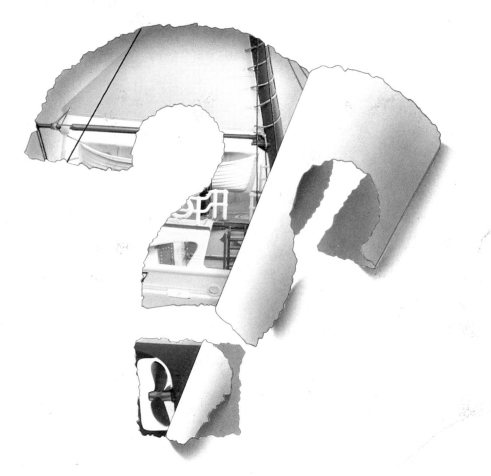

DORLING KINDERSLEY

LONDON • NEW YORK • STUTTGART

ROWING BOAT

This boat is for messing about on the river. It moves along when the oars are dipped in and out of the water. The rower pulls against the weight of the water to make the boat go forwards.

The flat, back end of a boat is called the stern.

Rowlocks are the U-shaped hook that hold the oars in place.

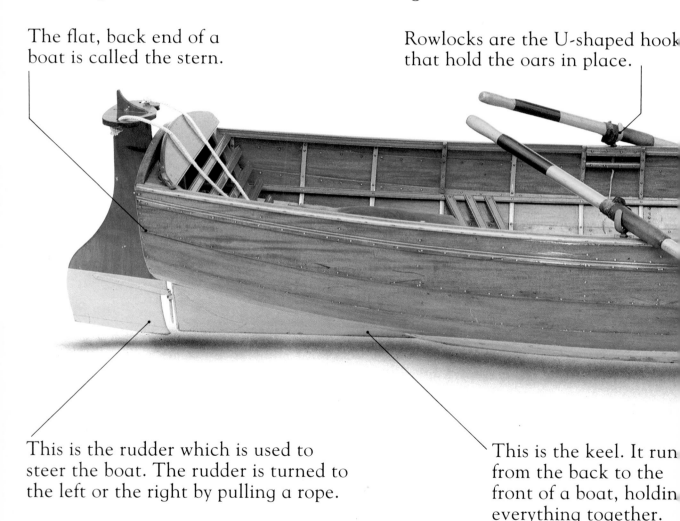

This is the rudder which is used to steer the boat. The rudder is turned to the left or the right by pulling a rope.

This is the keel. It run from the back to the front of a boat, holdin everything together.

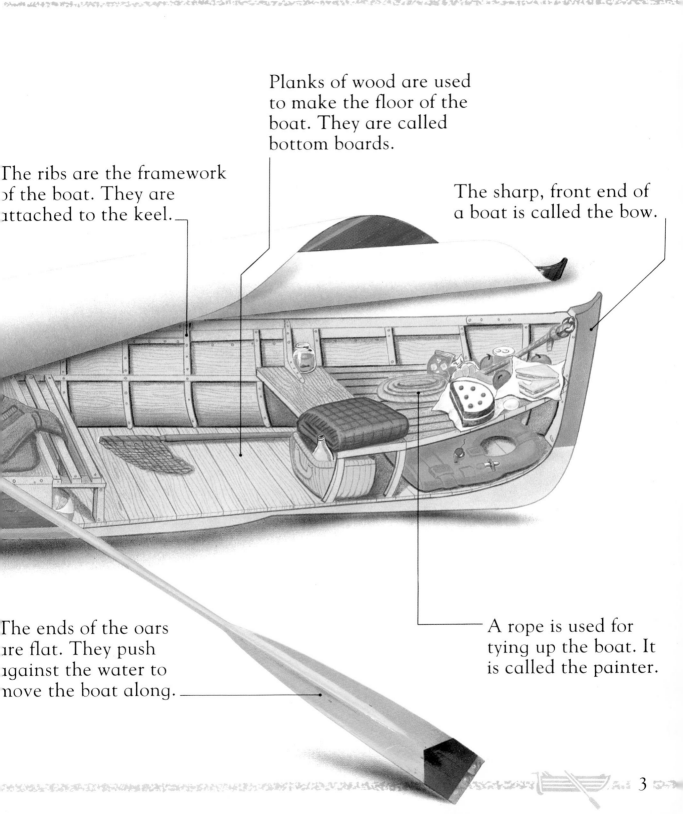

Planks of wood are used
to make the floor of the
boat. They are called
bottom boards.

The ribs are the framework
of the boat. They are
attached to the keel.

The sharp, front end of
a boat is called the bow.

The ends of the oars
are flat. They push
against the water to
move the boat along.

A rope is used for
tying up the boat. It
is called the painter.

CARGO BOAT

This is an old-fashioned cargo boat that once sailed up and down the Mediterranean coast, in and out of harbours and ports. It was loaded with barrels of wine, flour, fruit and other goods.

Lift up this hatch and you can go down to the place where the cargo is stored – in the hold.

This is the mas

When these big sails catch the win the boat moves through the water.

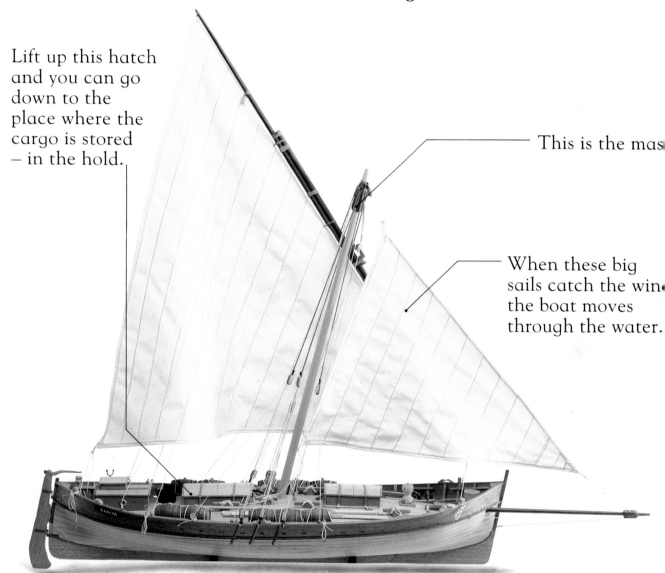

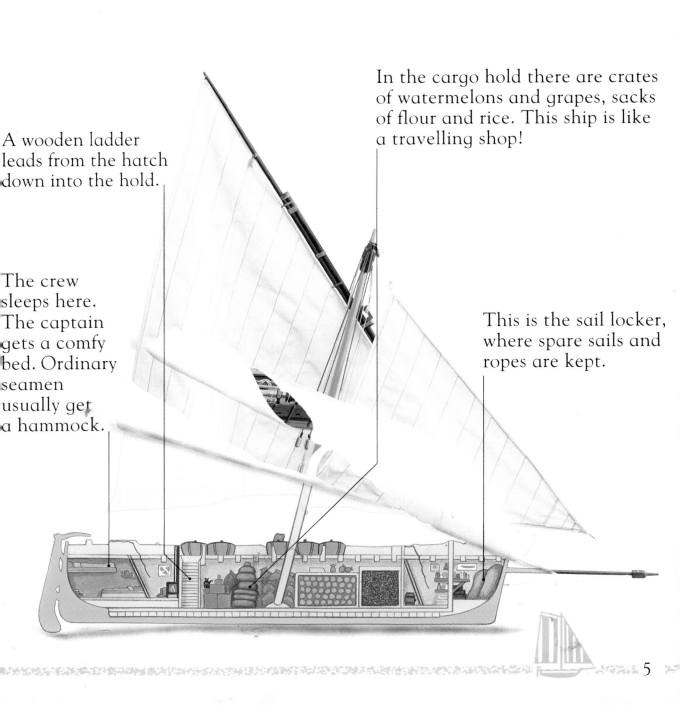

In the cargo hold there are crates of watermelons and grapes, sacks of flour and rice. This ship is like a travelling shop!

A wooden ladder leads from the hatch down into the hold.

The crew sleeps here. The captain gets a comfy bed. Ordinary seamen usually get a hammock.

This is the sail locker, where spare sails and ropes are kept.

RACING YACHT

This sailing boat is built for racing across oceans. It is long and thin. Its huge billowing sails catch the winds that send it speeding through the water.

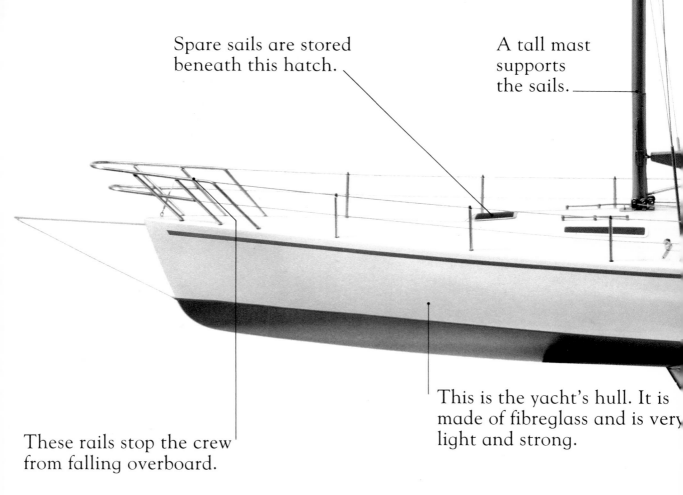

Spare sails are stored beneath this hatch.

A tall mast supports the sails.

This is the yacht's hull. It is made of fibreglass and is very light and strong.

These rails stop the crew from falling overboard.

The sails of this racing yacht are much bigger than the boat!

The crew members keep their clean, dry clothes in these lockers. Everything has to be stacked away very neatly to save space.

The bathroom is so small that you have to sit on the toilet to take a shower.

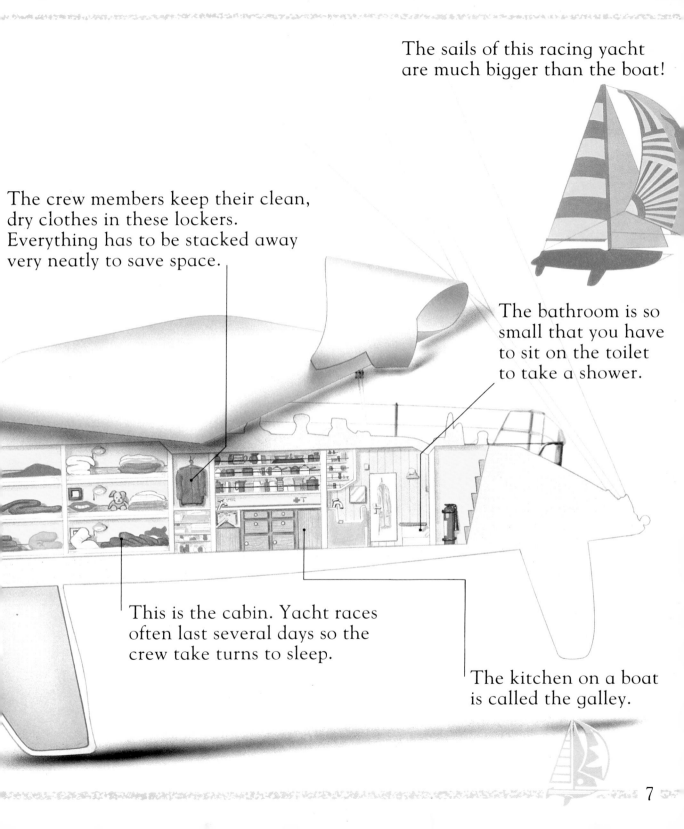

This is the cabin. Yacht races often last several days so the crew take turns to sleep.

The kitchen on a boat is called the galley.

FISHING BOAT

This fishing boat is out in storms and heavy seas every day of the week. It is called a trawler. It drags a big net slowly through the water, catching fresh fish for your supper.

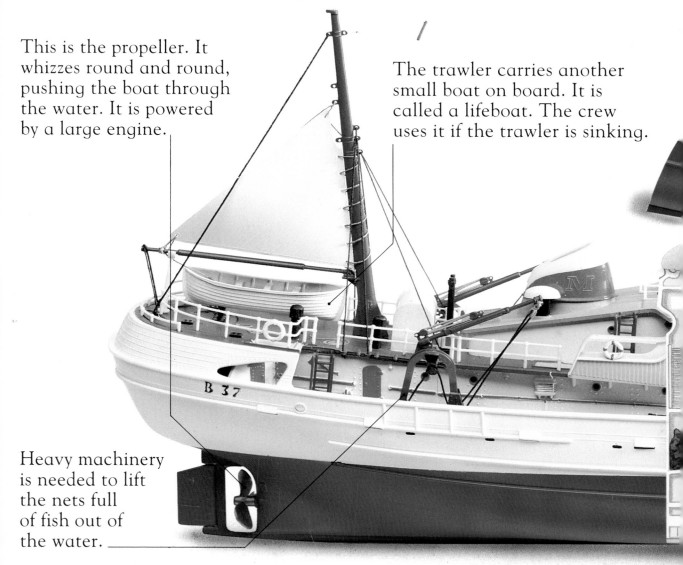

This is the propeller. It whizzes round and round, pushing the boat through the water. It is powered by a large engine.

The trawler carries another small boat on board. It is called a lifeboat. The crew uses it if the trawler is sinking.

Heavy machinery is needed to lift the nets full of fish out of the water.

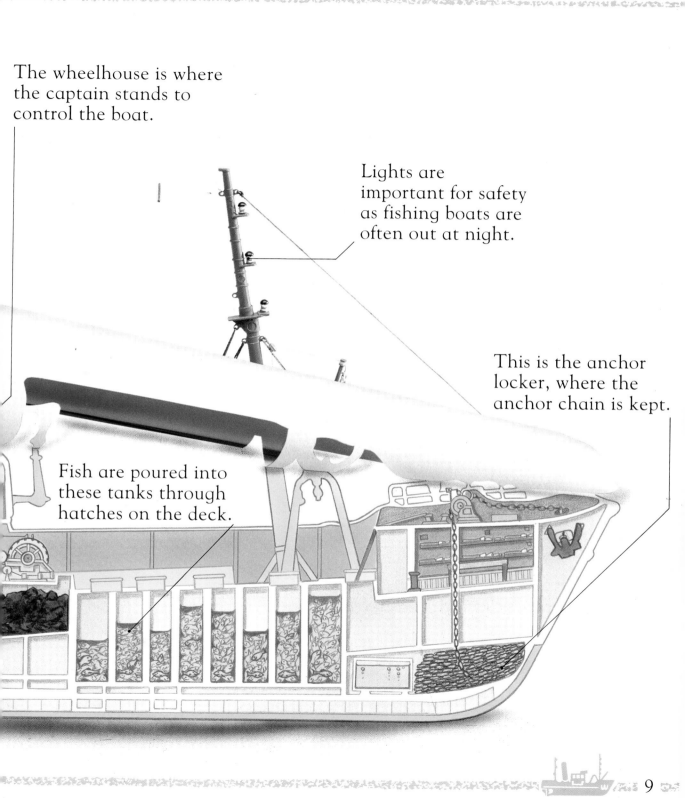

The wheelhouse is where the captain stands to control the boat.

Lights are important for safety as fishing boats are often out at night.

This is the anchor locker, where the anchor chain is kept.

Fish are poured into these tanks through hatches on the deck.

TUG

Tugs can be seen working in big ports and harbours. The job of a tug is to pull and push big ships in and out of their docks. To do this, tugs have to be very strong and easy to steer.

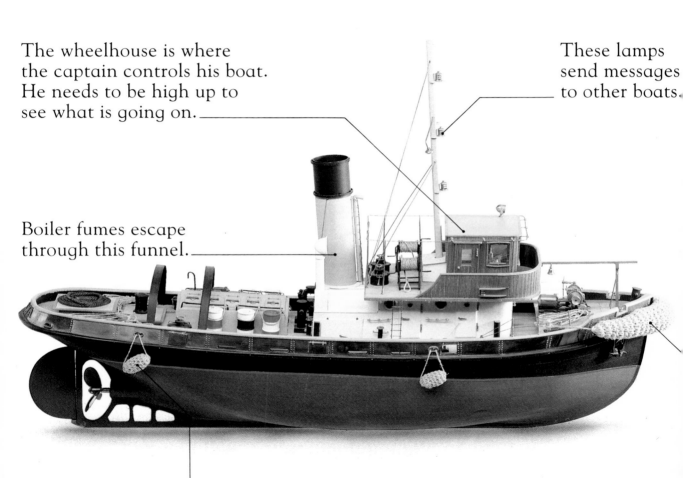

The wheelhouse is where the captain controls his boat. He needs to be high up to see what is going on.

These lamps send messages to other boats.

Boiler fumes escape through this funnel.

Fenders protect the sides of the tug from bumps and bangs.

Tugs do more pushing than pulling. With this big front fender, a tug can nudge a great big ship into the spot where it is wanted.

One tug pulls the ship and two others stop it from swinging from side to side.

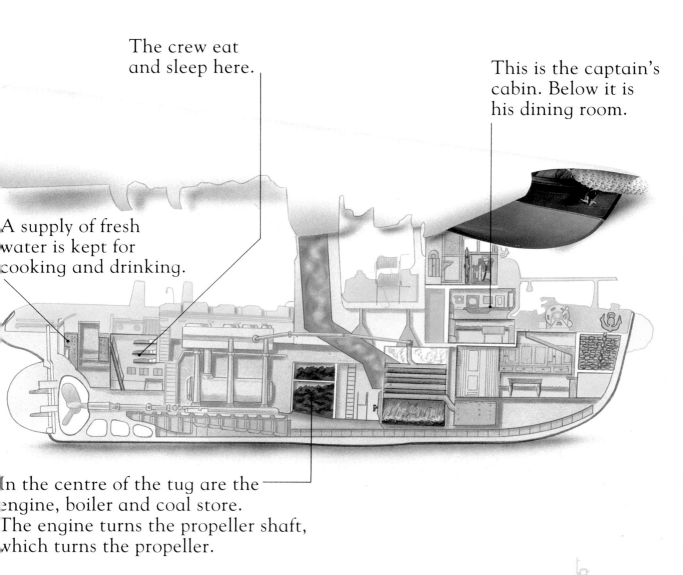

The crew eat and sleep here.

This is the captain's cabin. Below it is his dining room.

A supply of fresh water is kept for cooking and drinking.

In the centre of the tug are the engine, boiler and coal store. The engine turns the propeller shaft, which turns the propeller.

PADDLE STEAMER

Rivers were once major traffic routes, rather like motorways are today. A hundred years ago, boats like this steamed up and down the Mississippi river in America, taking people and cargo from one town to another.

As the paddle wheel moves round, the paddles push the boat through the water.

These cable support the funnels.

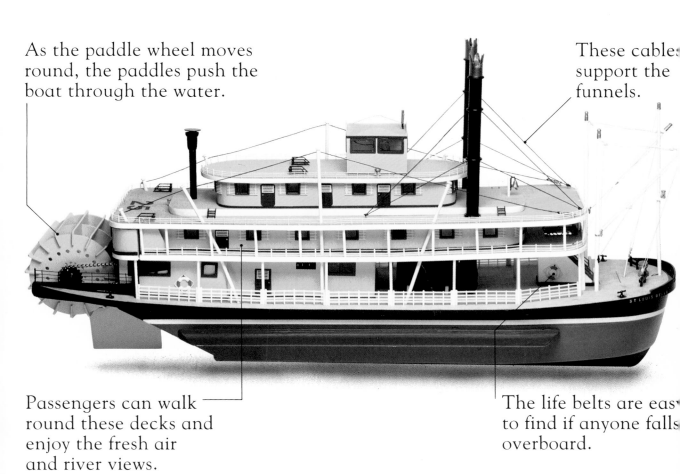

Passengers can walk round these decks and enjoy the fresh air and river views.

The life belts are eas to find if anyone falls overboard.

Some passengers only stay on board
for a few hours, just going to the next
town. Others travel for several days.

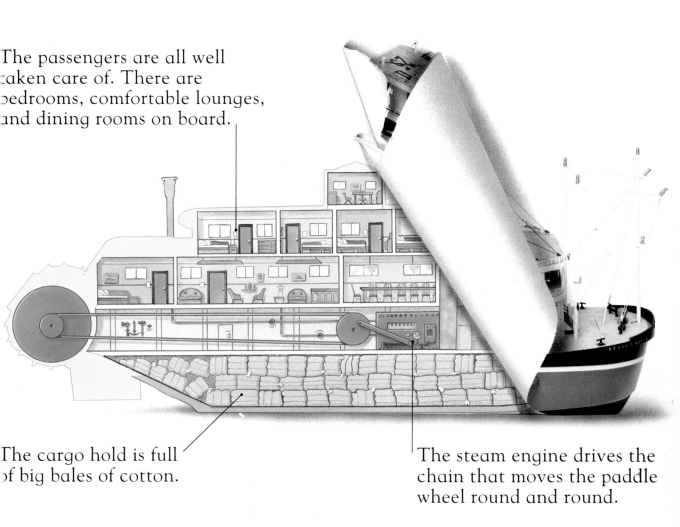

The passengers are all well
taken care of. There are
bedrooms, comfortable lounges,
and dining rooms on board.

The cargo hold is full
of big bales of cotton.

The steam engine drives the
chain that moves the paddle
wheel round and round.

LIFEBOAT

This boat saves lives. It can travel fast in bad weather and keep steady in stormy seas. Lifeboat crews are specially trained to rescue people from the sea and from sinking ships.

The hatches on deck are watertight so that all below stays dry in rough seas.

A boathook is used to reach out to small boats or people in the water.

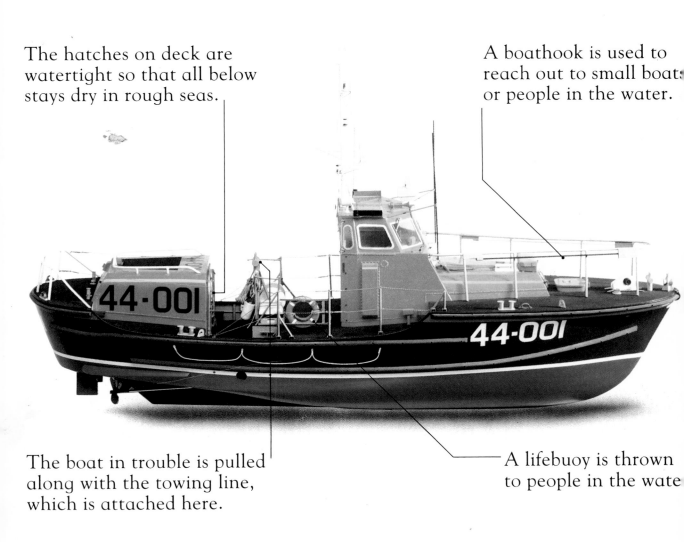

The boat in trouble is pulled along with the towing line, which is attached here.

A lifebuoy is thrown to people in the water

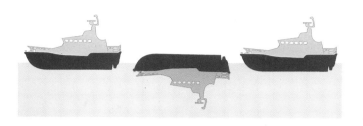

Lifeboats are very carefully designed so that if they turn over in rough seas, they are quickly able to turn back upright.

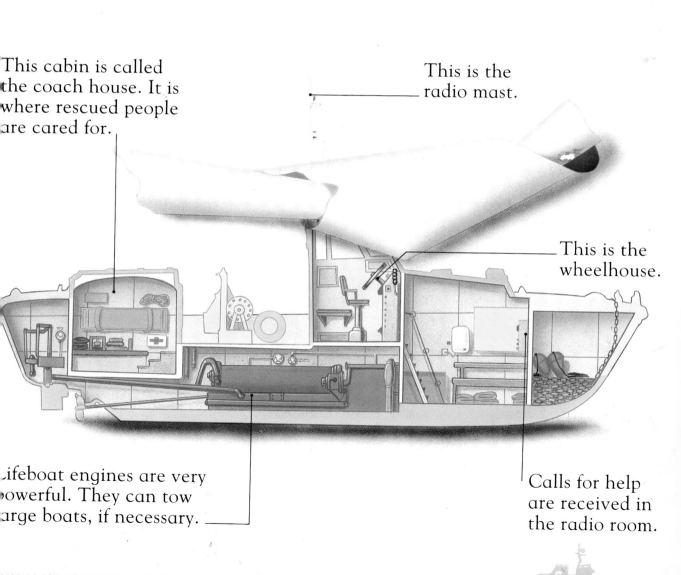

This cabin is called the coach house. It is where rescued people are cared for.

This is the radio mast.

This is the wheelhouse.

Lifeboat engines are very powerful. They can tow large boats, if necessary.

Calls for help are received in the radio room.

MOTOR YACHT

This boat is designed for cruising in the sun.
Guests invited on board will have nothing to do but
relax and enjoy themselves.

A speedboat can be lowered into
the sea for water-skiing, visiting
the shore or exploring beaches.

This is the bridge. When i
is raining, the captain sits
in here to steer the boat.

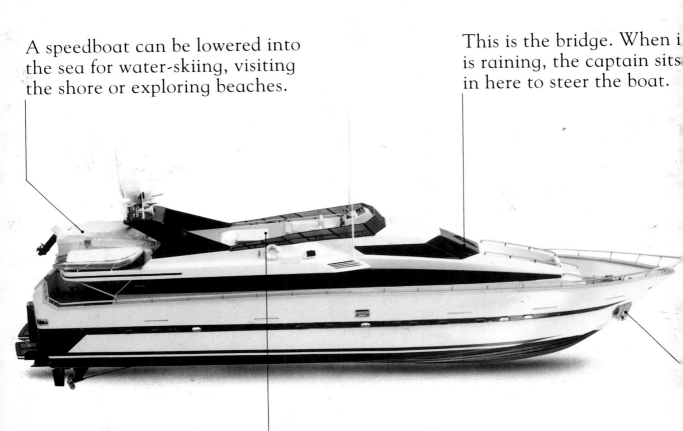

This open-top deck is where
the captain steers the boat
in good weather. The guests
can sit and sunbathe.

Here is the anchor. It will b
dropped if the guests want t
stop for a swim!